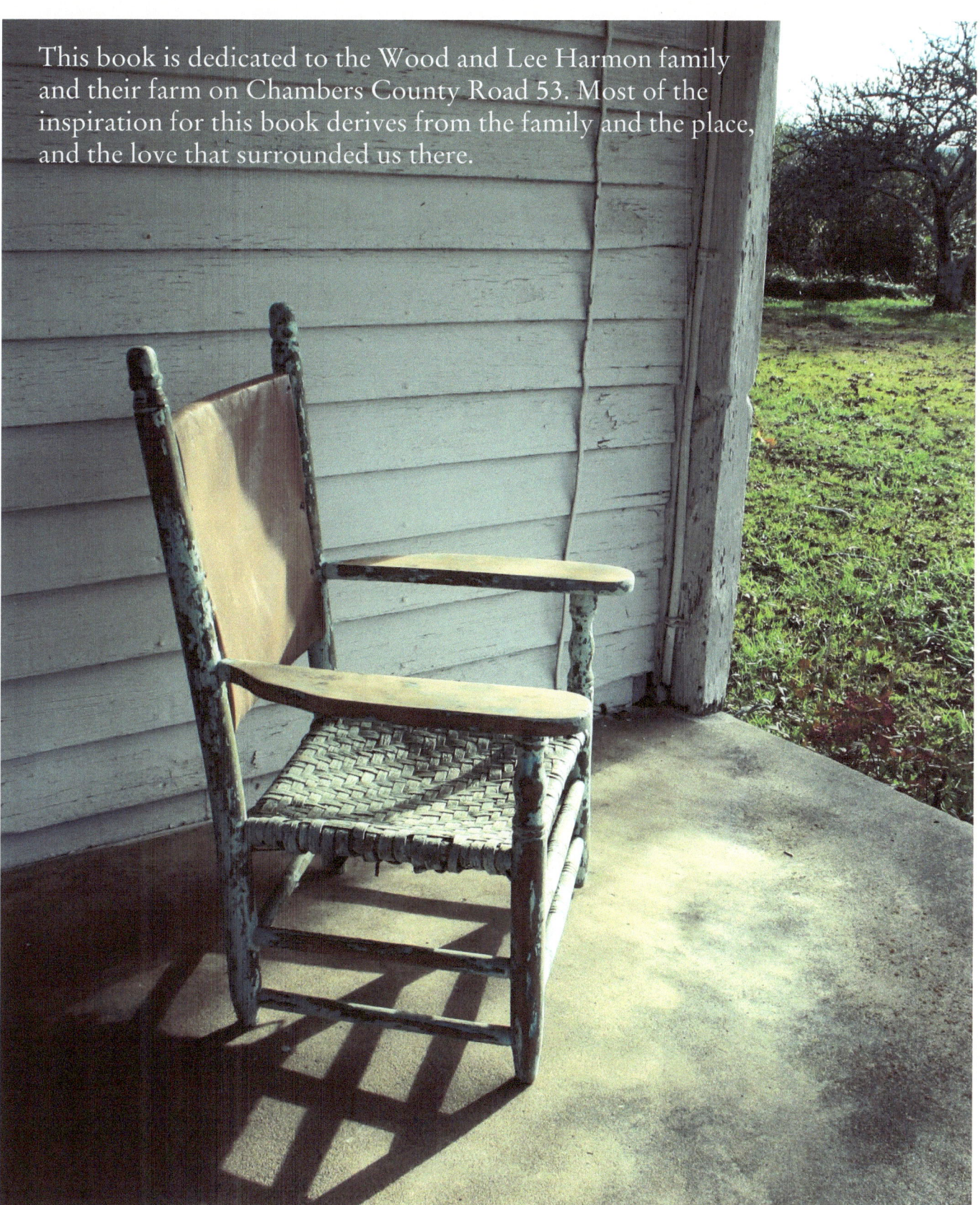

This book is dedicated to the Wood and Lee Harmon family and their farm on Chambers County Road 53. Most of the inspiration for this book derives from the family and the place, and the love that surrounded us there.

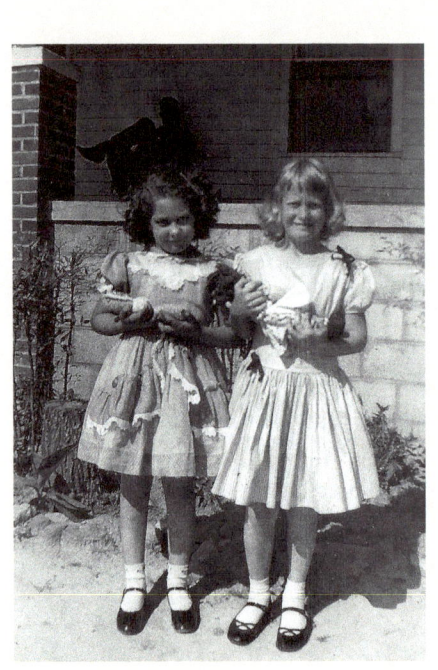
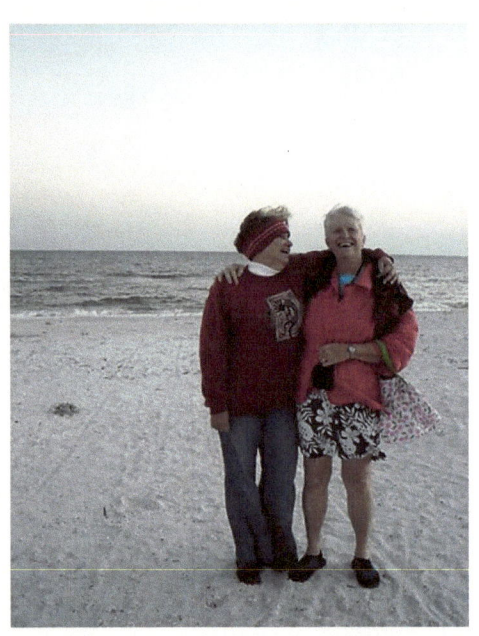

Photographs by Janice F. Sikes

A small Alabama textile mill village was the childhood home of Janice Foster Sikes. She had a natural bent for scientific matters and experimented on many household items, much to her parents dismay. She received a B.A. from Auburn University in Biological Science and Library and Information Studies. These degrees served her well as a public school educator.

A Master of Arts degree in Library and Information Science from UAB sealed her fate as a librarian. After retirement with thrity-three years of educational service, she continued to work as a reference librarian at a local public library. Presently, she is a math and science adult education instructor at Southern Union State Community College.

Photography became one of her passions, after observing her daughter 's photographic work. "I really wanted to take photographs like she did. So with her assistance, I learned the art and science of photography."

Sikes' photographic inspirations come from common everyday subjects viewed from an artistic perspective. Objects of natural and historical significance are also frequent themes of her compositions. She has four grandchildren, and they are the focus of much of her portrait work.

Poems by Crystal H. Rogers

Crystal was born in Chambers County, Alabama and grew up on a farm in the midst of an extended family. She learned about growing things on that farm: plants, animals, and relationships. Her mother spun out a stream of nursery rhymes and song lyrics that focused her attention from an early age on poetry and the beauty and comfort it provides.

She earned two degrees in math and science at Auburn University, married, and moved away from her beloved family and state. When her daughter and son were born she came back with her husband to the place she would always call home.

For the last 30 years, she has tended a family, her gardens, and relationships withher extendd family and friends. She has looked for meaning in events around her, and sometimes written about the things she observed. She recently began attending Osher Lifelong Learning classes and poetry workshops and began writing again after a long hiatus.

An empty house, an inchworm, or an old story remembered may be the material for a poem, a chance to extract a little more understanding from the world around her.

Photographs

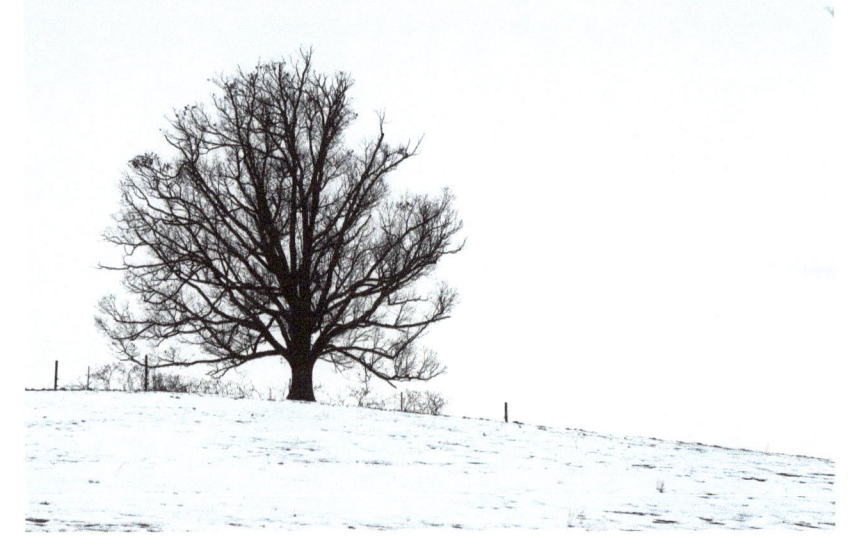

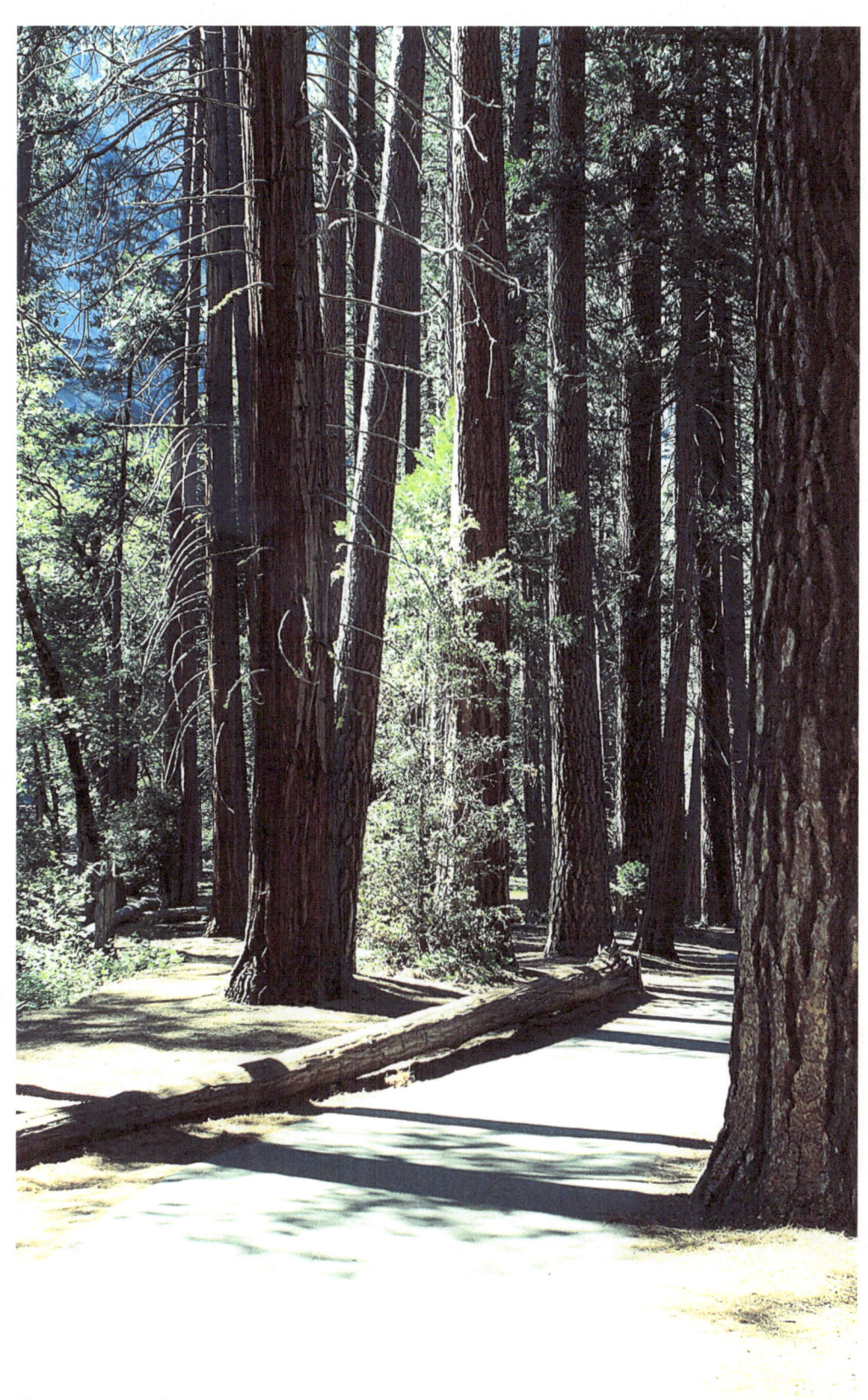

Cover Art & Design:
Julie S. Speir
Editor:r Hannah S. Rogers

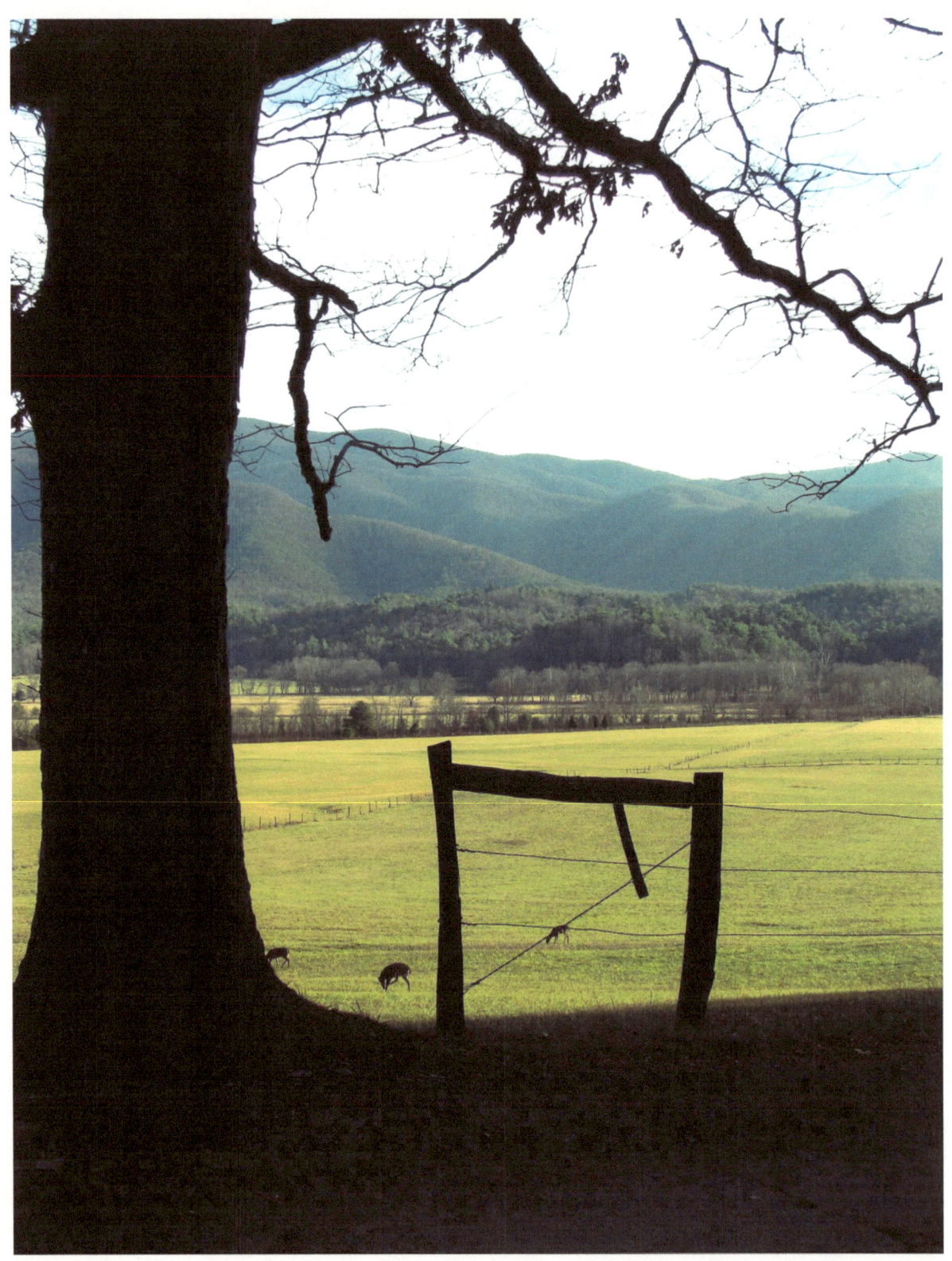

A Bath On The Steps

On the steps
of the abandoned house
She continued her bath,
She did not care who was
Watching.
The condition of the house
Did not bother her.
Nothing mattered
Except her bath and
The warmth of the sun.
She lifted one paw,
Licked it,
Used it to wash her face.
Her glance revealed
She was not afraid,
Had no interest in me.
She continued her
Grooming.
I reached out,
Half expecting her
To skitter away.
But no,
She accepted a scratch
To her ears
As her just due.
A few steps beyond her
Perch
Turning back,
She was gone.
Or was she ever there?

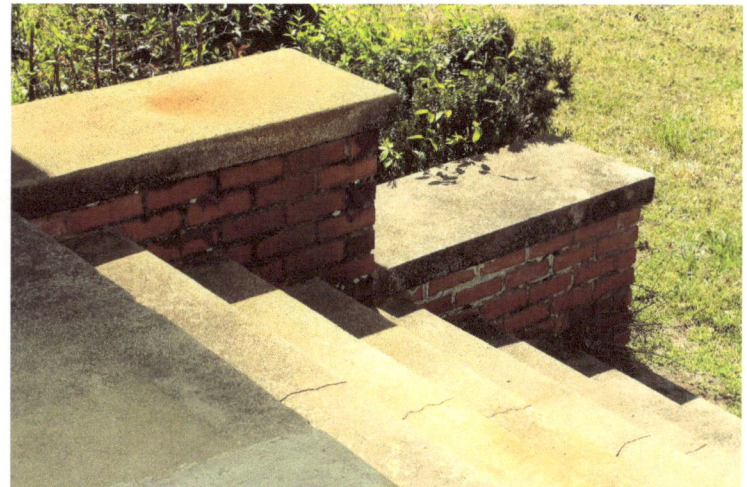

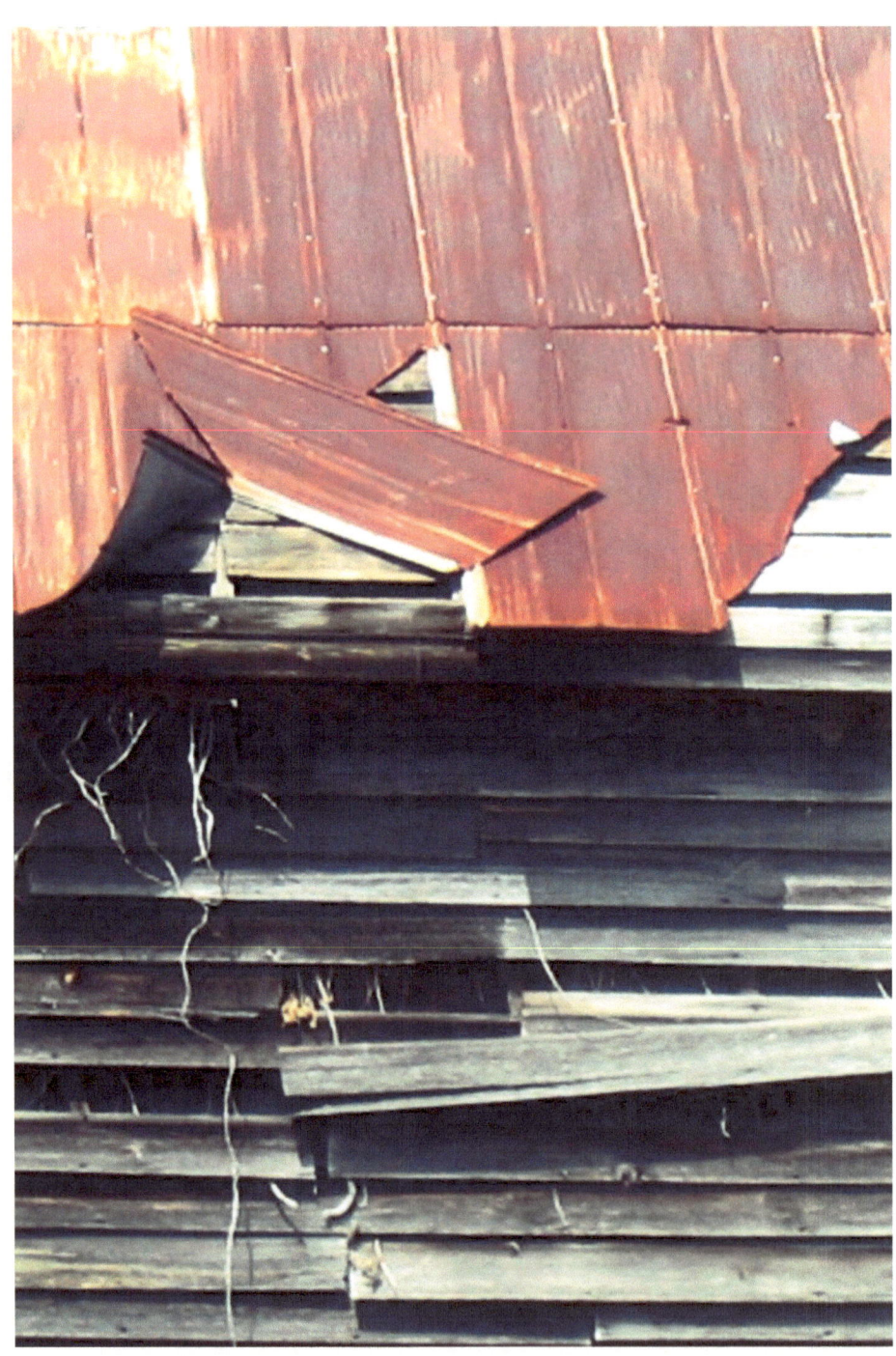

Spider Silk

A preying mantis
Turning his head
To see you better,
A black snake
On the steps
So startled he falls,
Dried up blueberries
Still clinging,
Clank of a bamboo chime
Warm bed in cold weathe
Baby kisses..

Turtle squashed on the road,
Her life mingled with tar.
Screech owl mourns
The loss of trees and creeks,
If she did not cry,
The rocks would..

A baby rabbit runs
Across the gardener's foot,
Thinks he is safe
beneath the bushes.
Unseen
Coyote's eyes gleam,
He yawns and stretches...

The preacher will not agree
with love of the temporal.
The lake reflects
Starlight,
Far away
Something splashes,
An owl calls
from the woods.

Inchworm

When I was least expecting it
You came to me,
Walking up my sleeve,
Chartreuse against navy.
Hurrying along
You picked up your head,
Looked all around,
Checked the territory,
Perhaps looking for me
Down goes your head,
Your rear quickly moves
Toward your head
Forming a loop.
Your head moves out
Again in a new step.
Wonderful and perfect!
But you are changing
into something different
Maybe better, Maybe not.
All life changes.
Right now is all we have.

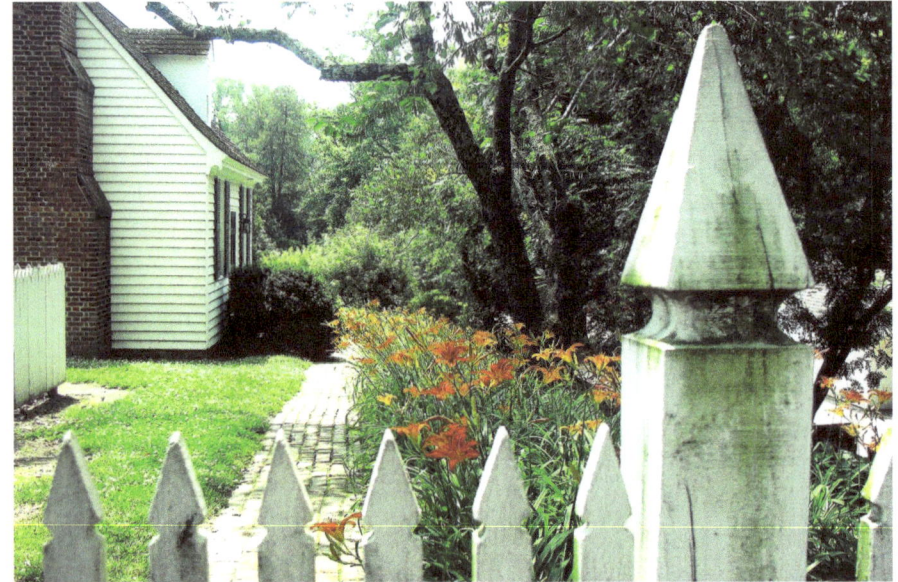

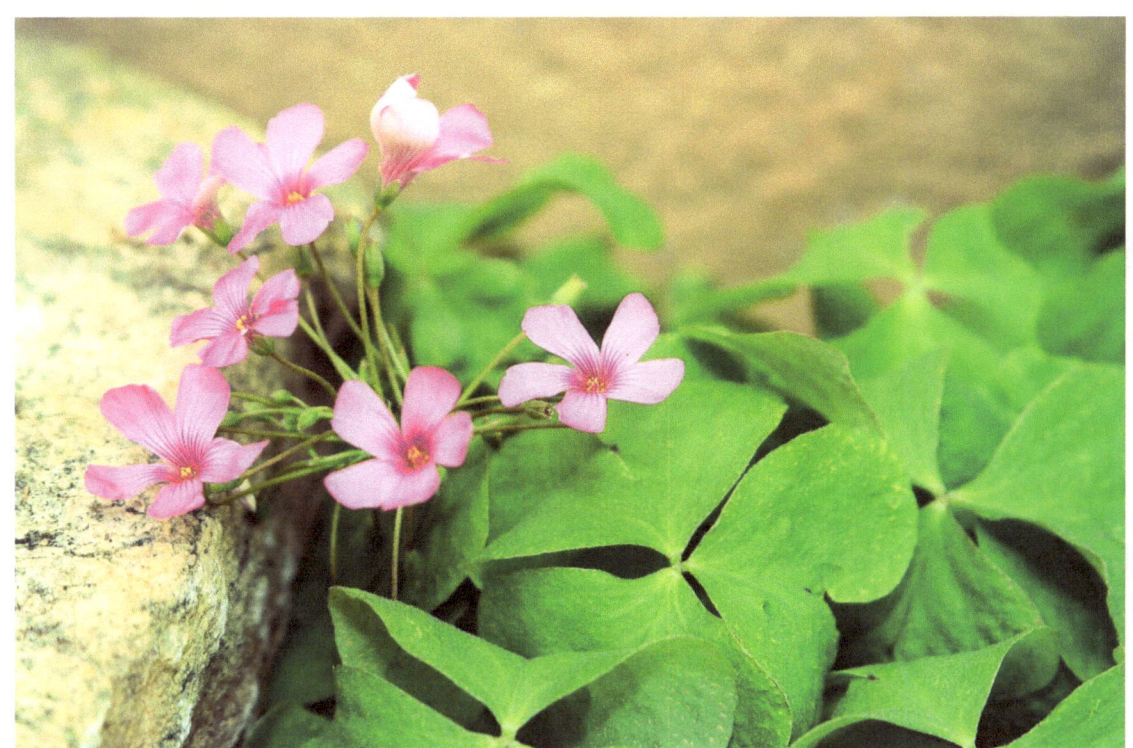

Mantis

Standing guard with folded hands,
She waits among the flowers.
Her turning head surveys the land,
She does not count the hours.
Her vision sharp, her aim is clear
Her arms held out so meekly,
Bee and moth need have no fear,
The end will come so quickly.
Face of mine look not so pasty,
She does not find you tasty

Snooks

Daddy Hubert
had a black cocker spaniel
whose name was Snooks.
Daddy got him
from a man named Snooks.

Every day Daddy
and Snooks
would ride over
to the store
to play dominoes.

One day
on the way home,
Daddy had to slam
on the brakes.
The sudden stop
Flung Snooks
to the floorboards.

Snooks looked up
at Daddy and said,
"What in the hell
did you do that for?"

Truthful Crows

Moral 1: Crows cannot speak
with forked tongue.
When my brother
was a boy,
He caught a crow
just learning to fly.
He put it in a cage
meant for a parakeet,
Much to the crow's surprise.

Our whiskey-breathed uncle
Told him the crow would talk
If he split its tongue.
He did.
Crow died.
Moral 2: People laugh at things
that are not funny.
Crows do not.

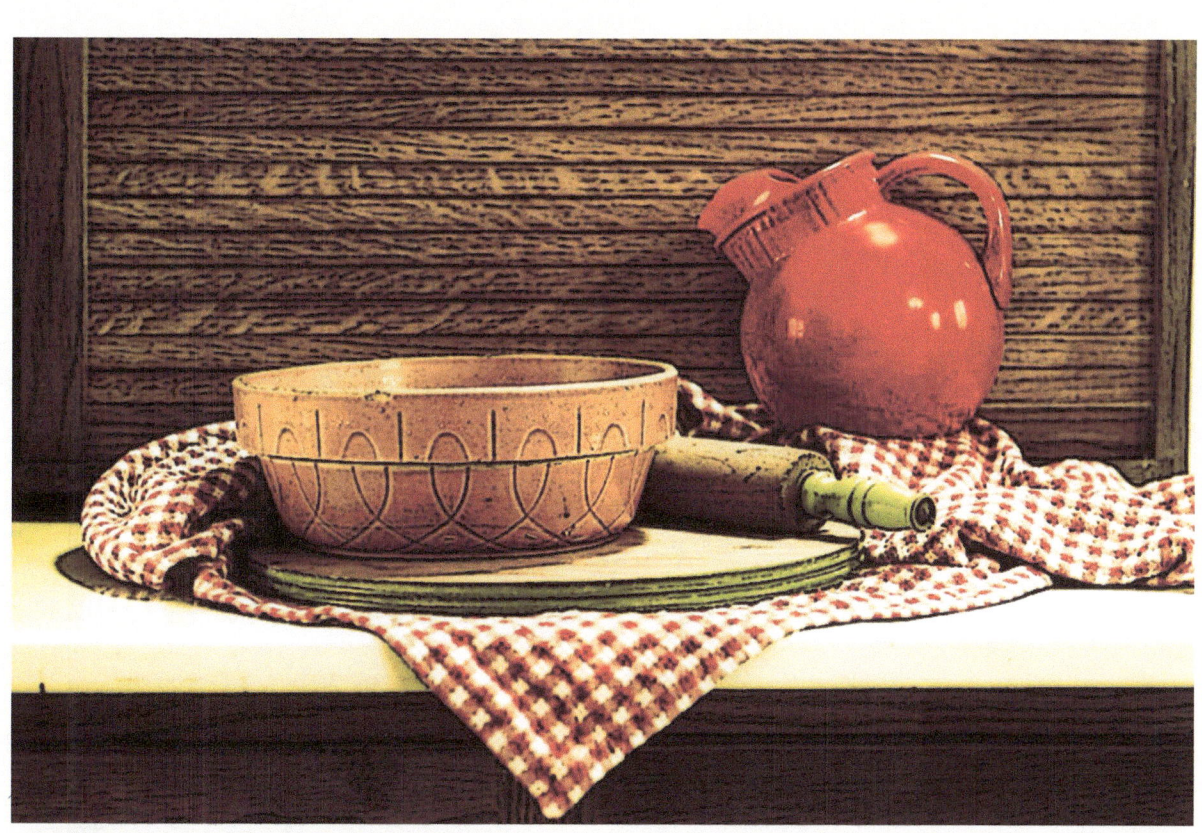

Nothing Concrete

A ghost town now
The place I grew up.
One after the other,
Emptied houses,
Stare vacantly at the road
Once dirt, now paved,
It could not save the place.

Farmers have taken their
places
In the cemetery.
Barns and houses crumble
Under the weight of years.

Youngsters have left
For computers, firetrucks,
And other shiny things.
It was too many hours
And too little money
And too much risk.

Tending mausoleums,
a heartbreak in progress.
Move along now.
And don't look back.
Leave it for the ones
Who don't remember.

The caretaker,
Stumbling along,
Praying these artifacts
Do not crash
On this watch.

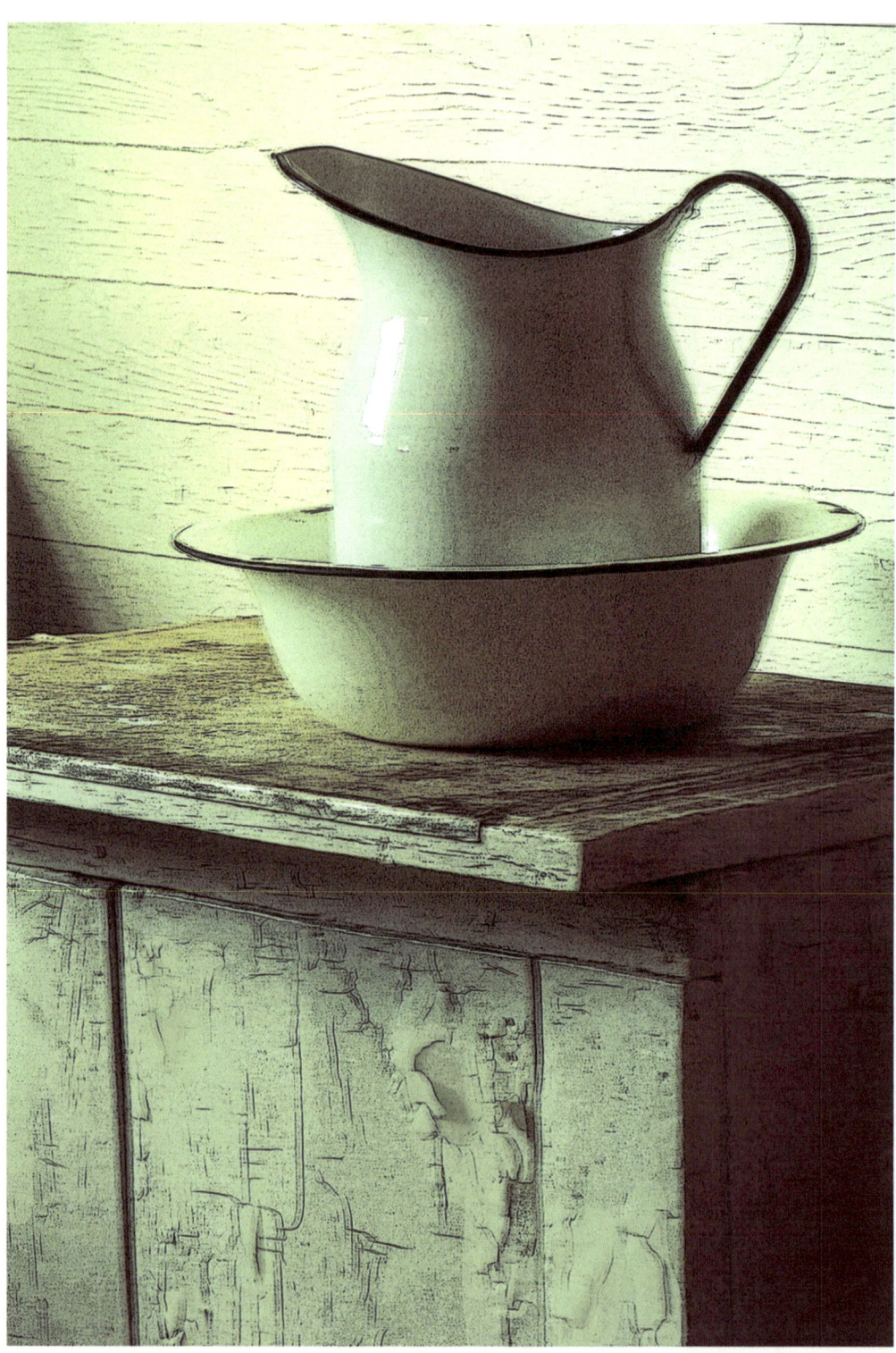

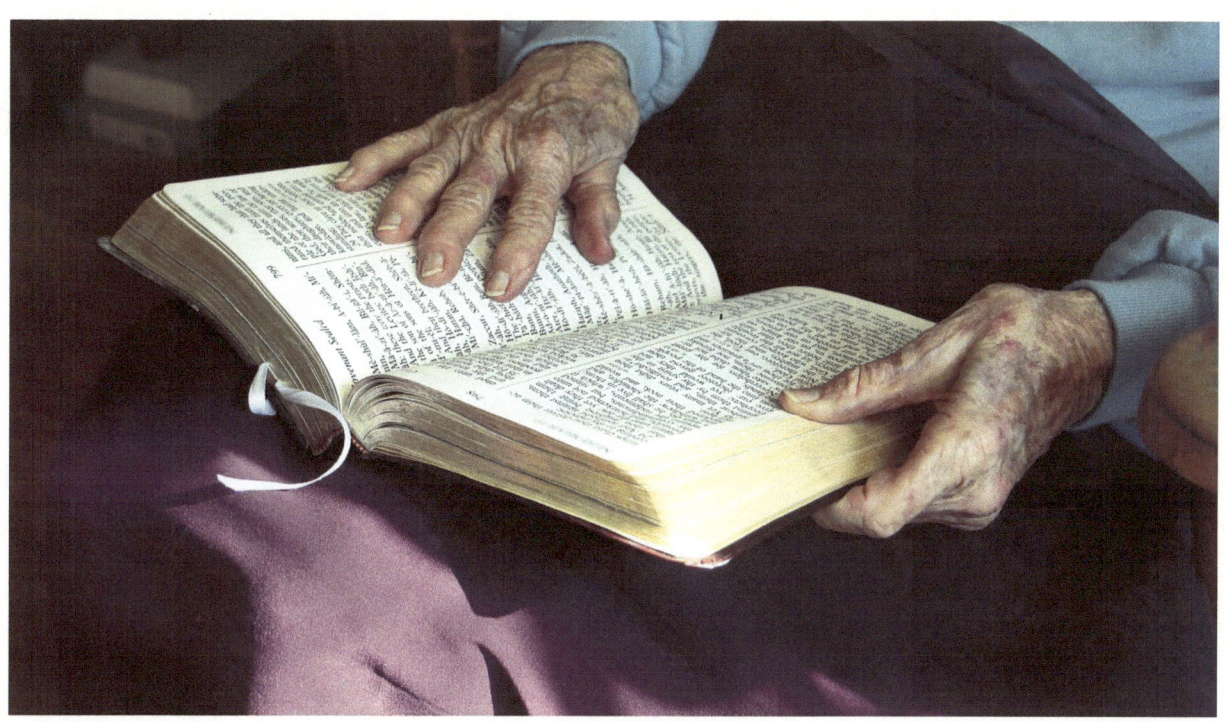

Thinking of Heaven

She wanted to talk about Heaven,
Sunny and 70 degrees,
R&B in the background,
Coconut cake,
Butterfinger blizzards,
Occasionally collards.
She didn't think much
of the golden streets idea.
She asked what I thought.
I misquoted some scripture
About wonderful things there.
She didn't want to hear that.
She wanted to think
About floating in the water,
Walking the beach,
Picking up shells.
If we could stay here,
there is no better place.

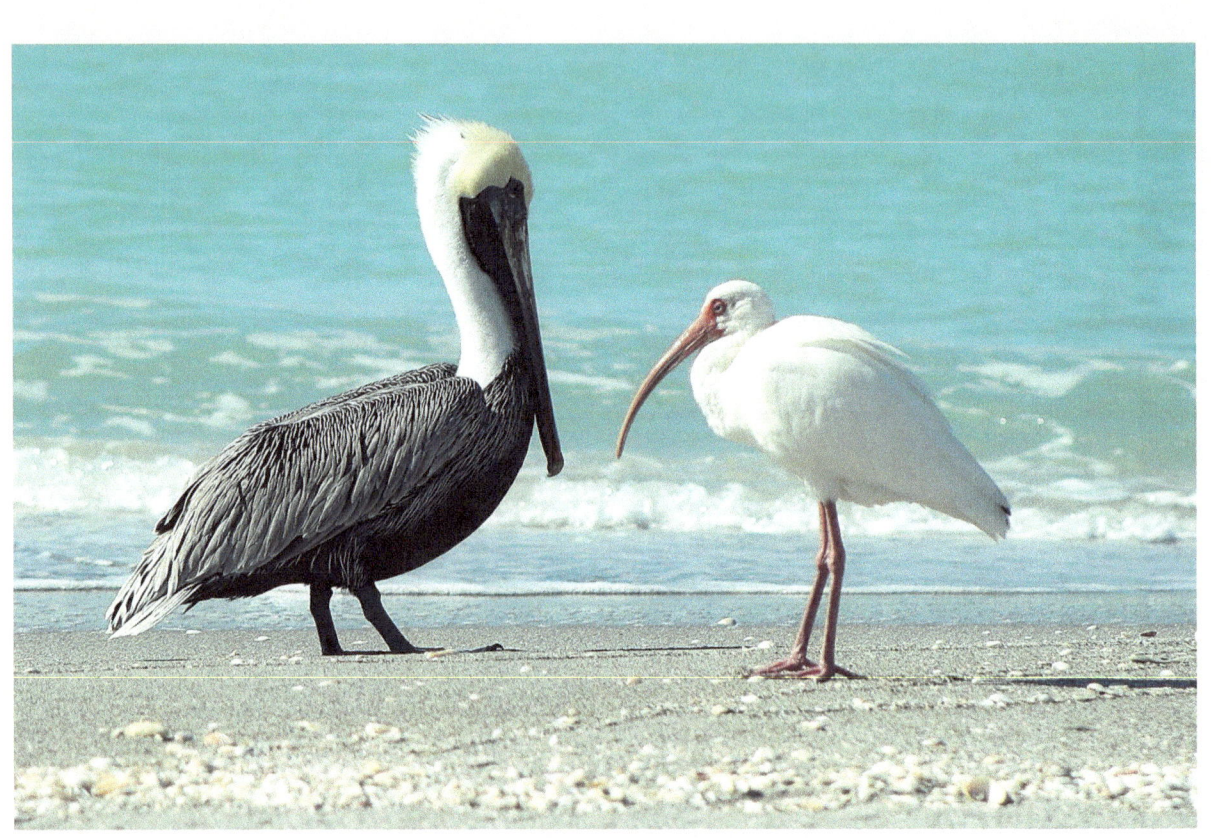

Dueling Roosters

Cock-a-doodle-do!
Wake up. all!
Beautiful day!
Cock-a-doodle do!

> Yes! Wake up!
> Sun's shining!
> I am the best.
> I am the most beautiful!

My comb is the biggest
And reddest.
My tail feathers are the tallest.
And most iridescent.

> Prowess is my middle name.
> I am the most fecund!
> My biddies are the strongest.
> They cover the earth.

Cover the earth?
Your biddies are as wretched
As their father!
Your hens are skinny,
Their feathers rumpled,
Their feet dirty.
They cackle like old ladies.

> You blind maggot!
> You cannot find one corn kernel
> Or one worm for your hens!
> You belong in a stew pot,
> Except you are
> Too old and tough.
> And, you talk too much.

You worthless Chanticleer!
If your own hens
Do not rise against you,
You will meet my talons!

> Fat Chance!
> Leave the safety
> Of your muddy pen,
> And I will peck your eyes out!

> Hush!
> Here comes breakfast!
> Lovely ladies, eat your fill.
> Sun's shining!

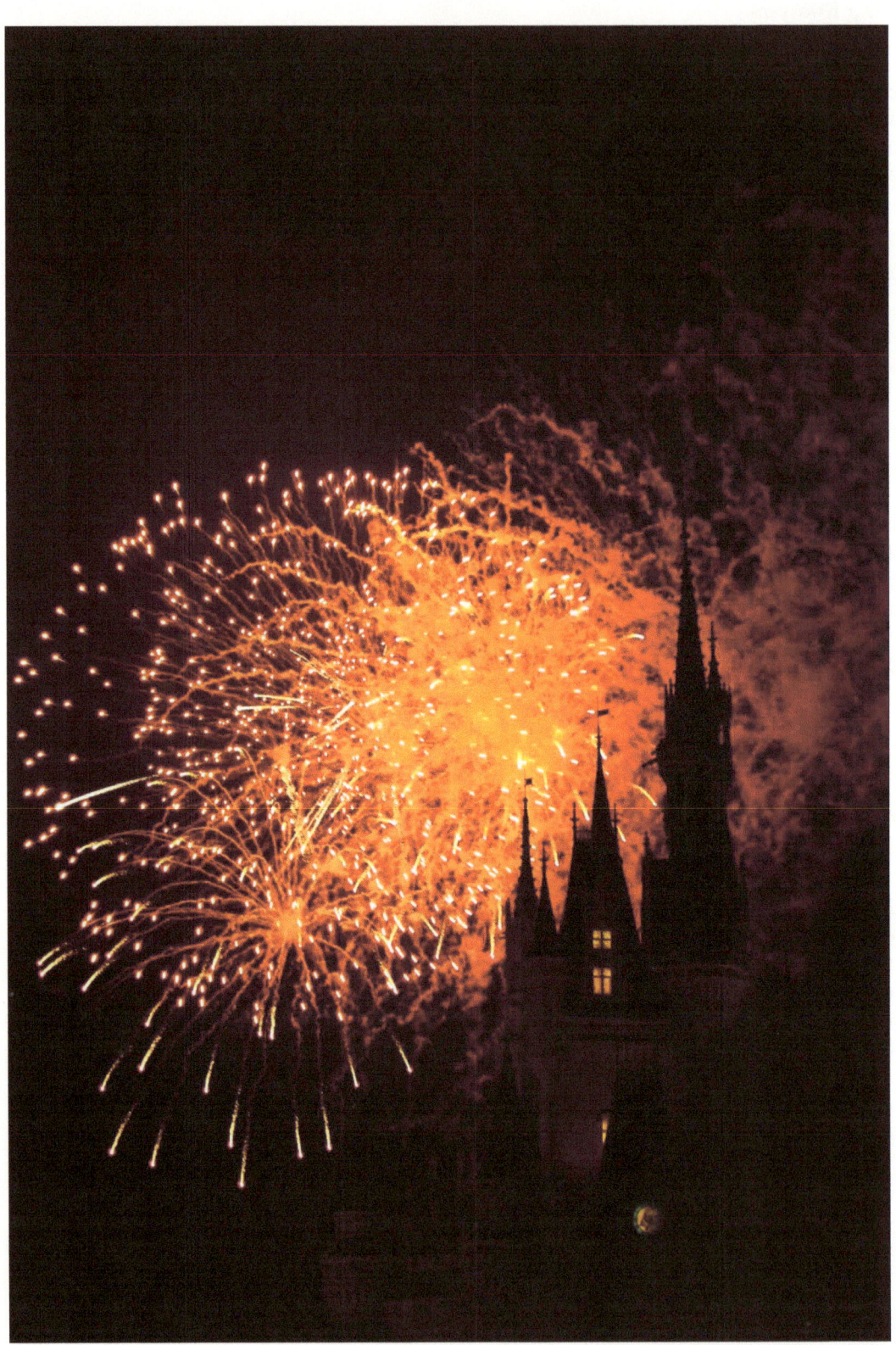

Reassurance

She seemed shorter than before,
I wondered if they had
Removed the bad parts of her back.
Her skin was smooth and clear,
Healthier than in years before.
We hugged for a long time,
Sat on the porch in the swing.
She said it was a motel,
where she stayed.
She said it had
tall white columns.
There were lots of trees,
with squirrels.
Lots of people came to see her.
She was calm, peaceful even.
She looked over the house,
familiar with all the changes.
I heard
what she told me.

Cold Quantum

If you were here
We would talk about
The coming storm.
The impossibility of doing
Anything about it,
Except to hunker down.
Then more pleasant topics,
Like funny hats in the catalog,
Mr. Green's truck passing again,
Aunt Zubie's travel stories,
That day at Pigeon Roost Bridge.
We would part
Happier, stronger,
More reconciled to fate.
Things I can't do alone.

Sleep

O Joy of Sleep,
That drops like a stone
Straight thru
To the gilded skies of morning.

No opening/closing windows
No lights on/off
No covers down/up
No dogs barking
No headlights on the wall
No exchanging bed/bed/chair
The rest of the damned.

Only a sweet black nothing,
Waiting the dew,
The breeze,
The first light,
The call of a new day.

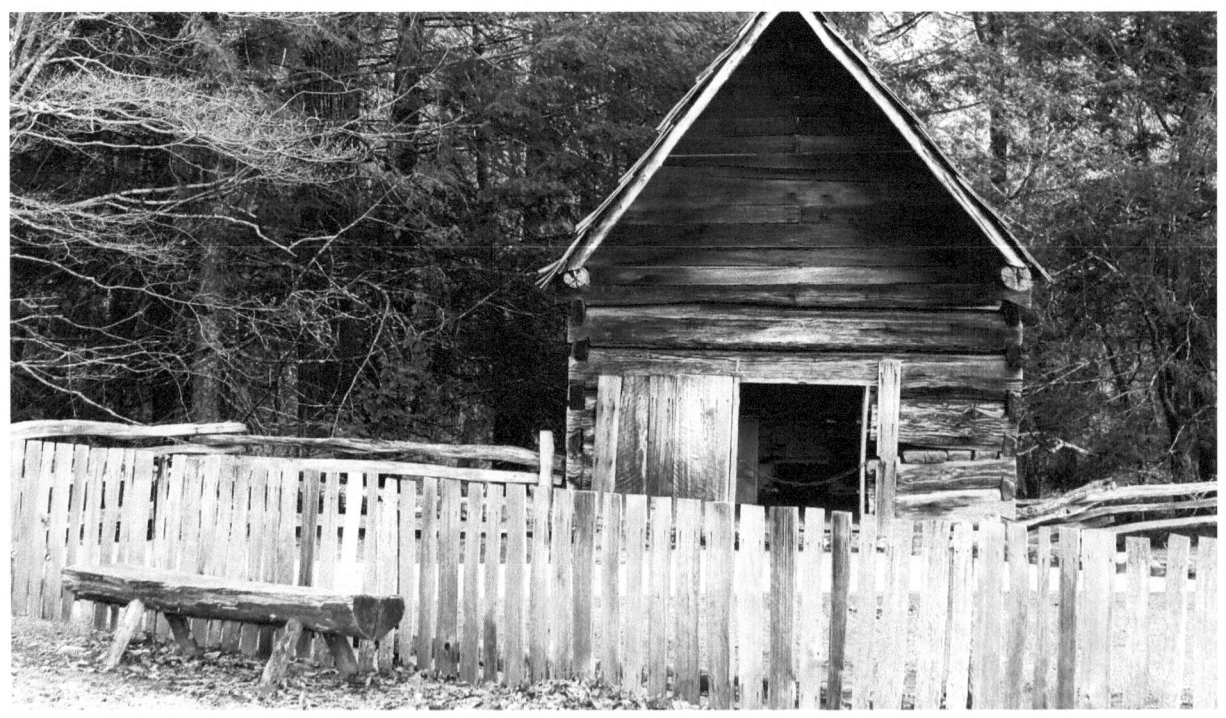

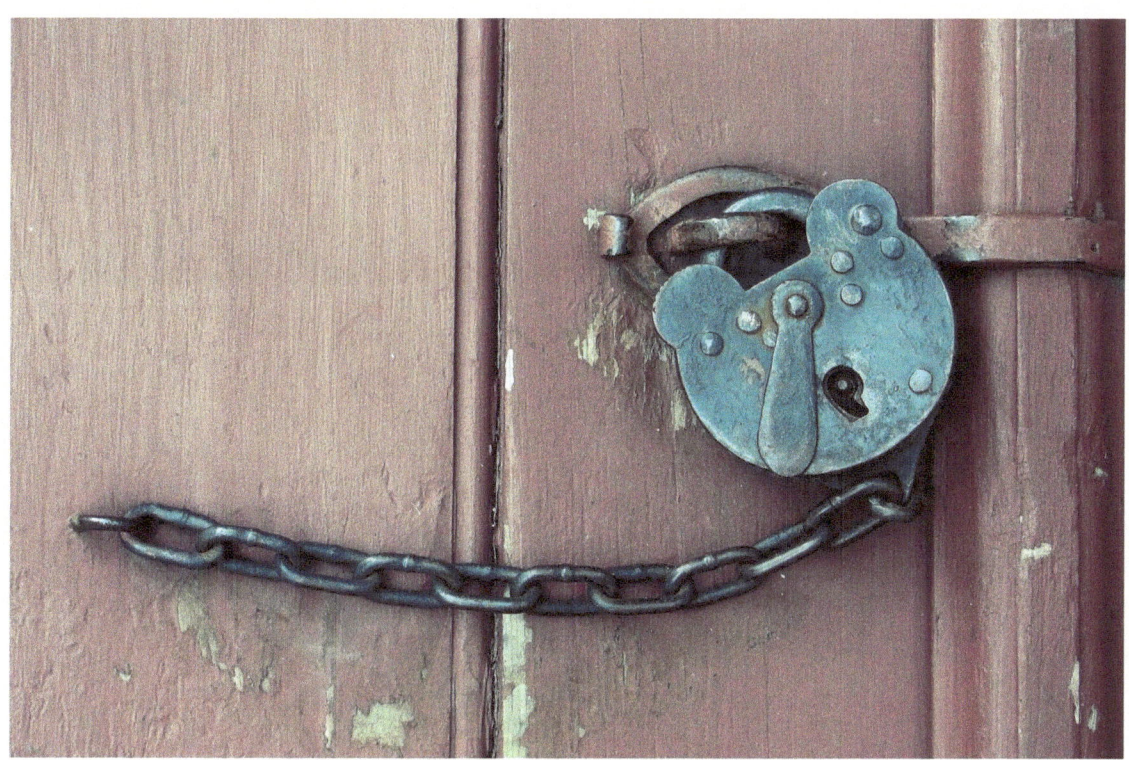

The Nightly Battle

About 8 o'clock
She starts to bark.
Her bark is thin and sharp,
A stiletto,
Making bubbles of pain
In the darkness
Calling, pleading,
Come out! Save me!
I need you! I'm scared!

The stabbing continues
Til, at the end,
I strap on my iron boots,
Grasp my light saber,
March resolutely
to her defense.

The bark dashes
into the darkness,
Ready for battle,
Sure of victory.

The iron boots stop
When the light saber's glow
Touches the edge of the woods.
Even I have limits,
Especially for an armadillo.

Chernobyl

Twenty years of snows
Have taken their toll.
Hole in the ceiling
Stares at the sky.
Underneath,
Roomy farm kitchen,
Electric stove, refrigerator,
Chairs shoved back
from a round table.

Classroom walls
still bright yellow,
Scattered books, desks
Speak a story
of hurried departure
and loss.

In the field,
Combine rusting,
Tractor tires
Flattened and sinking,
Barn sagging sideways,
Stall doors banging
in the wind.

Bushes alive
with birds,
once shot
and poisoned,
Now the dawn
brings a cacophony
of fecund joy.

Carefully engineered
Drainage ditches
Beavers turned
Into something
They can use.
Wolves return
to their ancestral home,
Growing fat
on their new beaver diet.

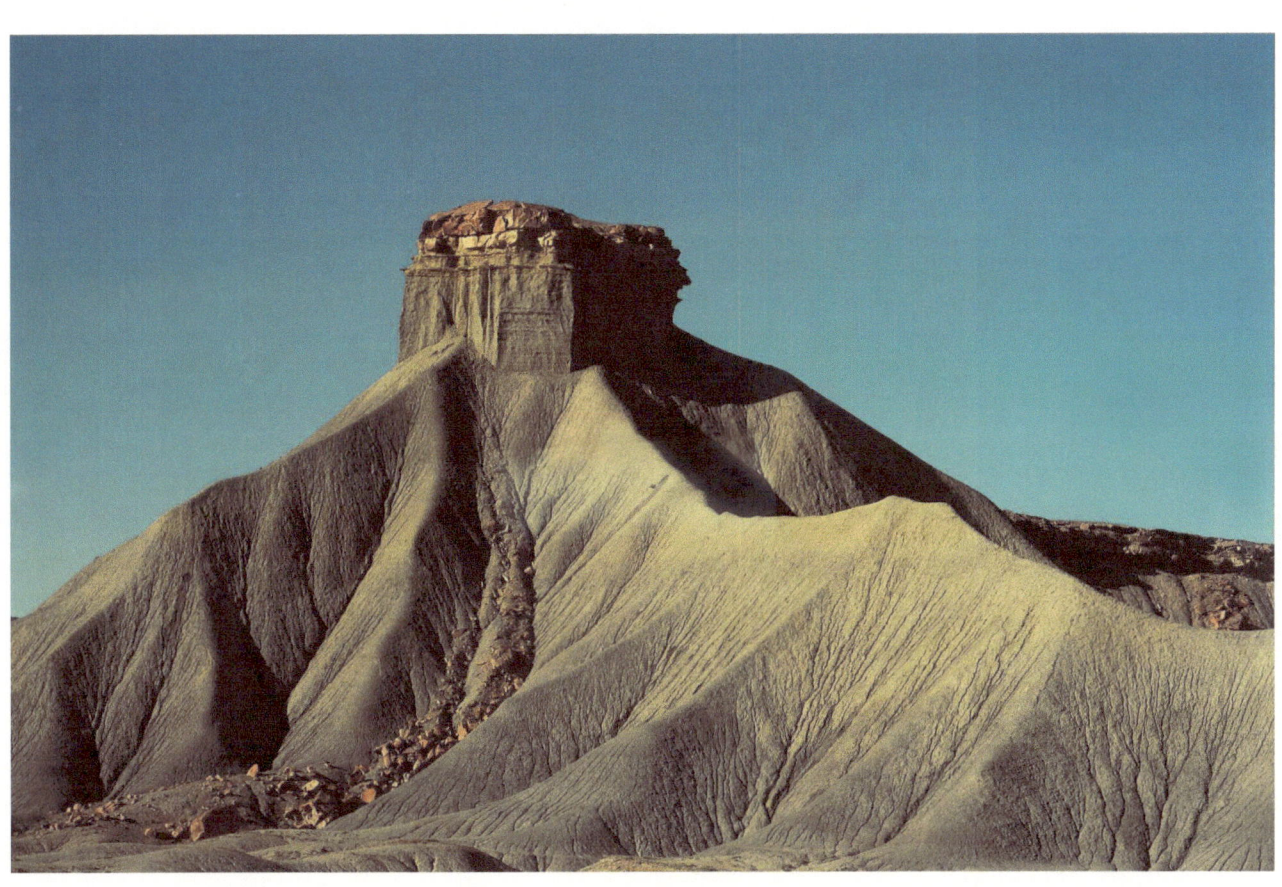

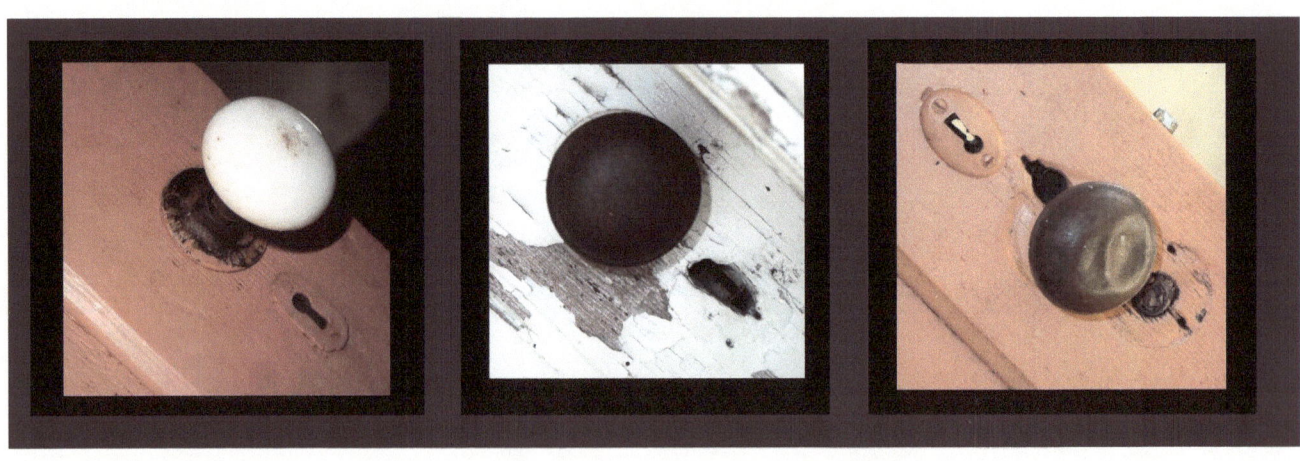

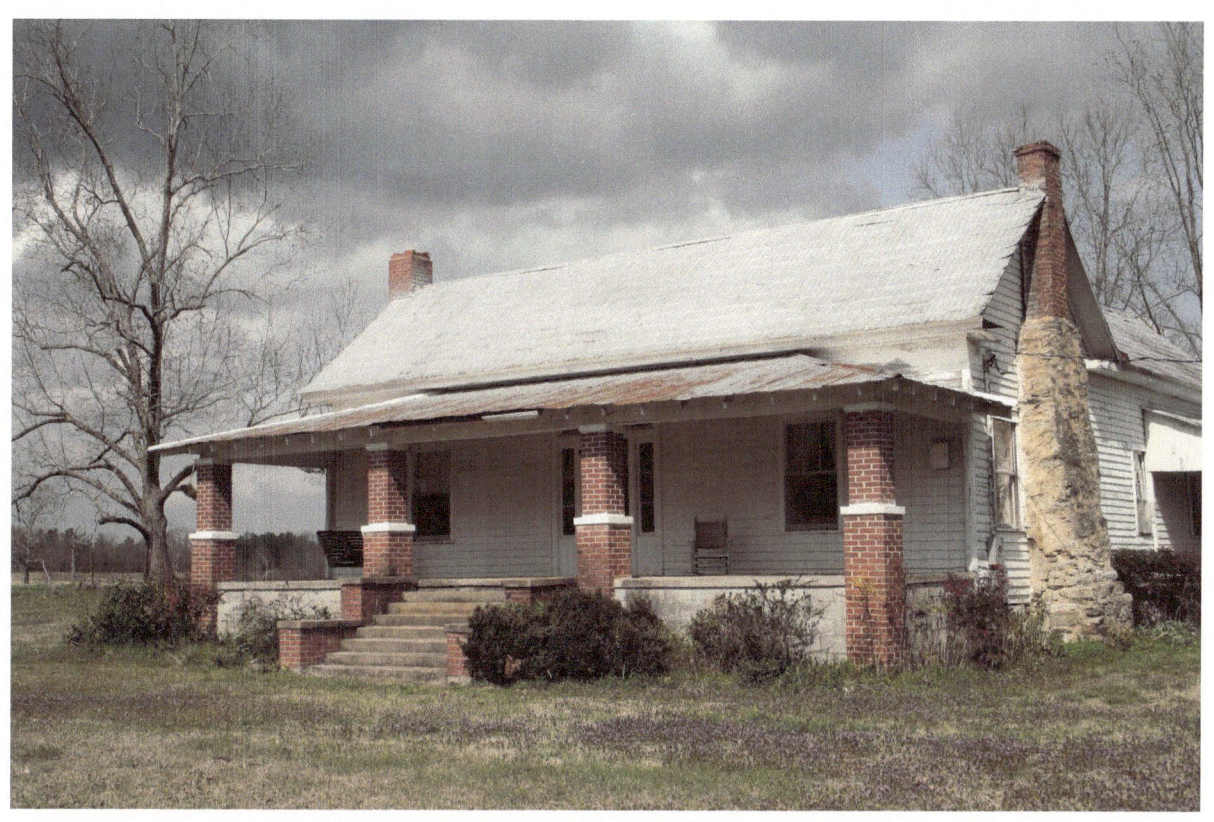

Spoon By Spoon

We eat our lives

Bite after bite,

Till the spoon

Scrapes bottom.

Afterward

Only memory,

Unless

We did not

Notice.